Ethical Dilemmas and the Practice of Diplomacy

Charles Ray

Uhuru Press
North Potomac, MD

The opinions contained in this book, except where they have been specifically attributed to an individual or institution, are the opinions of the author, and are not meant to represent the policy of the US Government or any institution, organization, department or agency thereof.

The reproduction or distribution, by any means, including electronic distribution, is expressly prohibited without the written consent of the copyright holder, except for fair use quotes in connection with reviews.

For information about this and other works of this author, contact the author at charlesray.author@gmail.com.

Printed in the United States of America

Cover design and interior illustrations by the author.

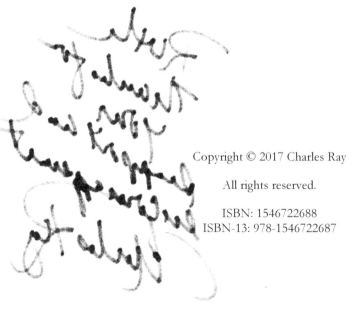

Copyright © 2017 Charles Ray

All rights reserved.

ISBN: 1546722688
ISBN-13: 978-1546722687

DEDICATION

To the memory of Mary A. Ryan (1940-2006), who served as the Assistant Secretary of State for Consular Affairs from 1993 to 2002. A mentor and friend to many in the U.S. Foreign Service, Mary was someone who 'walked the talk.' And, to America's 'First Line of Defense,' the men and women of the U.S. Foreign Service who live the words of John F. Kennedy's January 20, 1961 inaugural address; 'ask not what your country can do for you – ask what you can do for your country.'

ACKNOWLEDGMENTS

The list of people to whom I owe a debt of gratitude for their encouragement, assistance, and inspiration, is far too long to be included here. There are those, however, who simply have to be included.

My grandmother, a woman of limited education, but profound intelligence, who inspired me to reach for the sky; my mother, although afraid to fly—she never in her life traveled by plane—taught me how to conquer my fears; and Paulyne Evans, my first high school home room and English teacher, who recognized the writer in me long before I did. These three women established the foundation for all that I have accomplished in life.

Susan Johnson, president of the Association for Diplomatic Studies and Training (ADST) in Arlington, VA, when she was the president of the American Foreign Service Association (AFSA), gave me the opportunity to explore the role of ethics in diplomacy. It was under her leadership that AFSA's now defunct Committee on the Foreign Service Profession and Ethics was formed, and even though it didn't survive long enough to accomplish all its aims, it got the conversation started; a conversation that continues.

I also want to thank the colleagues, active duty and retired, from all the foreign affairs agencies, who served with me on the PEC from 2012 to 2016. They were willing to share their time and experience, listen politely to an old man's war stories, and just as politely, tell me when they thought I was off base. While the PEC no longer exists, the motivation behind it lives on in the hearts and minds of those in the Foreign Service who realize that a culture change in the service is long overdue.

Foreword

During Charlie Ray's exceptional career in the U.S. Foreign Service and the U.S. military, he developed an appreciation for the role of leadership, management and ethical behavior in the constellation of sustained performances required to execute successful U.S. foreign policy. Previously Ray has written incisively about leadership and management and this present volume takes on the important, all too often neglected, subject of ethical dilemmas in the practice of U. S. diplomacy. It focuses on identifying and dealing with the gray areas of ethical behavior, the need for ethical thinking to be infused throughout diplomatic careers and the need to reform the way the State Department and the Foreign Service approach ethics for diplomats.

As former Director General of the Foreign Service I can attest to the commitment and dedication of the U.S. diplomatic workforce and am well aware of the many ethical dilemmas that our colleagues must deal with during the normal course of a career. Ray's observations offer a succinct road map to help these good people avoid making bad choices. He employs excellent practical examples with just the right focus on the positive aspects of ethics and he helps the reader by providing thought provoking discussion questions. Ray concludes with important recommendations for institutional changes that would provide diplomats with more support and better tools to handle ethical dilemmas. Moreover, it is an enjoyable read that will help to equip our diplomatic corps for success in today's turbulent world.

Ambassador Ruth A. Davis (retired)

*Ruth A. Davis served as Director-General of the U.S. Foreign Service and Director of Human Resources for the U.S. State Department. Prior to her **retirement** from the Foreign Service, she was confirmed for the rank of Career-Ambassador, the highest rank in the Foreign Service.*

PREFACE

I entered the Foreign Service after 20 years in the army, with extensive experience in security and foreign cultures, but zero knowledge of diplomacy—in that last, I was not unlike the vast majority of Americans. I was determined, though, to learn as much as I could.

During a 30-year career in the Foreign Service, I learned a lot.

Through observation and practice, I learned the fine points of diplomatic practice, and through reading, the history of American and international diplomacy. As might be expected, I viewed a lot of this from a military perspective. I brought with me from the military an interest in leadership, and from the lessons I learned at my grandmother's knee, a commitment to ethics and integrity. It was only natural, therefore, that for much of my diplomatic career these two issues would be at the forefront of my mind.

I've written previous books and articles about leadership. In this book, my focus is on ethics. Not, mind you, because I think there is an ethics or integrity problem in the Foreign Service—at least no more than might be found in any government organization, including the military. My Foreign Service colleagues, in the main, were some of the most honorable people I've ever encountered. As in any organization, though, there will be a few bad actors, but these are mostly dealt with by the existing regulatory structure. I say mostly, regrettably, because on occasion during my 30 years of service, I witnessed occasions (admittedly rare) of people committing ethical lapses and going unpunished. That too, unfortunately, happens in every organization.

While these ethical lapses concern me, I'm even more concerned by the lack in government of training and mechanisms to help people deal with what I call ethical dilemmas. These are not the cases of legal vs. illegal, but are what John P. Friedman, in the Association of the American Foreign Service Worldwide (AAFSW) book, *Realities: Foreign Service Life, Volume 2*, described as 'gray areas of issues when there are no absolute rights or wrongs.' When I retired from the Foreign Service in 2012, I accepted the position of chair of the Committee on the Foreign Service Profession and Ethics (PEC) of the American Foreign Service Association (AFSA). The PEC was charged with developing an ethical code of conduct for the Foreign Service, and one of the main areas of emphasis was developing mechanisms to help people deal with these 'gray areas.'

While the State Department and the other foreign affairs agencies have comprehensive compliance ethics programs, none of them address the issue of ethical dilemmas, so the PEC was essentially starting with a blank slate. This would be a formidable task even with the full support of the affected organizations behind it, but what I discovered during my two years as chair of the PEC was that there seemed to be little interest in going beyond the current regime of compliance ethics. In fact, AFSA disbanded the PEC in the summer of 2016, for reasons that were never clear to me, and little has been done on this issue since in any formal sense.

It is with that in mind that the idea for this book was born. I believe that helping people deal with situations where the choice is between two courses of action where there are no absolute 'rights or wrongs,' is just as important, if not even more important, than ensuring compliance with the legal prohibitions of the compliance ethics system. In fact, when people have a good sense of how to deal with the gray areas, it's been my experience that they deal even better with the compliance issues. When they know how to make decisions when the choice is not between legal versus illegal, the gray areas become less murky.

During my career in the Foreign Service, I noted on a number of occasions, a disparity in how ethical violations were handled. Some employees, when they broke the rules, suffered maximum punishment, while others—sometimes in the same organization and under the same supervisor—suffered no punishment at all, even when they broke the same or a similar rule.

I want to stress here, that my focus on this subject is in no way meant to impugn the integrity of the Foreign Service or the vast majority of its members. Admittedly, there was the occasional rotten apple—I encountered them in the military as well—but, the people who flagrantly violated the rules were extremely rare. What I did encounter frequently, though, and the thing that troubled me greatly, was the apparent lack of awareness of the impact that the gray areas of ethics, or the dilemmas one must contend with when faced with two 'legal' choices, and the lack of acknowledgment of this issue by the training system. Other than the annual ethics orientation, often a rather amateurish video that is more boring than enlightening, and required acknowledgement that one has viewed it, ethics was not a subject of conversation routinely engaged in during my diplomatic career—and, as far as I can ascertain, still isn't.

If the United States is to have a truly professional and competent diplomatic service, this, among other things, is one thing that has to change. We live in an era of uncertainty, and the dangers our country faces cannot be dealt with by military force alone. We are also in a time of policy confusion and moral/ethical ambiguity, requiring that our diplomatic representatives, when dealing with confused foreign audiences, be able to explain American policy and politics honestly, while living up to our oath to 'support and defend the Constitution against all enemies, foreign and domestic.' They must know where their ethical 'line in the sand' is drawn, and how to deal with situations that, while not illegal,' might challenge personal ethical standards.

With that in mind, I offer the reader my thoughts, as well as results of research I've done on the issue, in the hopes that the discussion we'd hope to inspire in 2012 when we formed AFSA's Committee on the Foreign Service Profession and Ethics will finally take place.

INTRODUCTION

On Saturday, December 8, 1981, I overslept.

It wasn't unusual for me to sleep in on weekends, sometimes not crawling out of bed until 9:00 am to play with my son and daughter, ages 7 and 6, to make up for all the missed time during the week. At the time, I was the senior language training advisor for Slavic languages at the Defense Language Institute, Presidio of Monterrey, California, which meant a lot of late hours during the week. Often, the kids would be in bed by the time I got to our house on Fort Ord, which was about six miles from the Presidio. On this particular morning, though, I had a special reason for getting out of bed early.

In September, I'd applied to take the Foreign Service Officer Test (FSOT), and had received my admission ticket to take it on December 8 at a high school in San Jose. The distance from Fort Ord to the school was about 60 miles, about an hour and a half up US 101 under ideal traffic conditions. If I remember correctly, the test was scheduled to start at 9:00 am, which meant I needed to be pulling out of my driveway no later than 7:00 am. The problem; I woke up at 6:30.

My wife, who is something of a pessimist, grumbled when I shot out of bed, took one look at the clock, and advised me to crawl back under the blanket and forget it because there was no way I could make it in time. Now, that's precisely the wrong thing to say to an East Texas farm boy. I put my mind in red alert mode. I set the coffee perking while I showered, shaved and dressed in record time. Clutching a hot mug of coffee in one hand while driving with the other, I backed out of our carport at 7:24. I stayed well within the speed limit as I drove across Fort Ord to the exit to Seaside, the blue-collar town to our north (the MPs on base had a zero tolerance for speeders), pushed it to five miles over once I left the base, and then rammed the gas pedal to the floor once I hit 101.

That was both smart and stupid at the same time. Just outside the town of Seaside, I hit a wall of fog so thick I could barely see ten feet beyond the front of my car. On the one hand, that meant unless the California Highway Patrol was doing radar speed monitoring I wasn't likely to be seen and ticketed for speeding. On the other hand, it meant that I risked running my car under the back of an eighteen-wheeler unseen in the fog until I was almost on top of it. But, I was determined to make it to the test center in time, so I said a little prayer, and kept my eyes glued to the space in front of the car, hoping I'd see at least a glow of taillights before I smacked into someone.

Since I'm writing this over thirty years later, you know I made it. In fact, I arrived at the test center with a whopping four minutes to spare, and a few weeks later I received a notice in the mail that I'd passed the written test and was invited to appear for the Oral Assessment in San Francisco in January. There was less drama for that segment of testing. I drove up to San Francisco the day before, checked into the guest quarters at the Presidio of San Francisco, and did a driving recon to determine where to go, where to park, traffic conditions, etc. A well-executed military operation that came off without a hitch, and, by the way, I passed the oral as well, and was invited to join a Junior Officer Orientation Class (known as the A-100 class for its numerical designation on the curriculum) at the Foreign Service Institute (FSI) in Rosslyn, Virginia, on August 10, 1982.

Thus, began my Foreign Service career, a career that spanned just over thirty years, and took me to some of the world's most exotic locations—at least to an East Texas farm boy they were exotic at first, but within a very few years became, in fact, very routine.

After A-100, I did the Consular Orientation Course, known as ConGen Rosslyn, which introduced new Foreign Service Officers (FSOs) to the laws, regulations, customs, and procedures of consular work, which is what we were all expected to do for our first tours when I joined. We spent three weeks learning about visas, passports, jail visits, birth registration, and citizenship adjudication, with practical exercises and role play to reinforce classroom learning. Even though I'd spent a lot of my adult life abroad by that point, with army tours in Germany, Vietnam, and Korea, and had a foreign-born wife and two children born abroad, I was still amazed at how involved the process for a foreigner to travel to the United States actually was. In fact, despite having worked with embassy folks in Vietnam and Korea, and having applied for my wife's immigrant visa and certifications of birth and passports for my children, I realized on the first day of ConGen Rosslyn, that I had no idea what went on inside an embassy or consulate. Part of this, I realized about midway through my career, was (and still is to a degree) due to the reluctance of FSOs to discuss what they do with outsiders or the public, part to the lack of recruiting and advertising by the Foreign Service or the Department of State back then, and a large part to the lack of awareness of many Americans about what

American diplomatic and consular personnel do for us on a daily basis.

It was in interesting revelation which set me on a course to learn more, and moreover, do something about it, but more on that later.

After consular training, I spent six months in language training, gaining a rough knowledge of spoken Mandarin Chinese. Now, useful Chinese can't really be learned in such a short period of time, but under the regulations of the time, untenured FSOs and first-tour officers were only allowed six months of language, regardless of the difficulty. I had a bit of an advantage over some of my colleagues, though, having learned Vietnamese through a year's study before my first military tour in Vietnam, and picked up basic German and Korean during my tours in those countries. In fact, I managed to test at 2/2 in Vietnamese, and 1+/1+ in German and Korean, and by the end of six months got a 2+/2 in Mandarin.

These ratings are an assessment of a person's ability to speak and read the language, with the first number rating the skill level in speaking and the second in reading. The ratings range from 1 for elementary proficiency to 5 for native or bilingual ability. The level 2 is considered limited working proficiency, 3 is professional working proficiency, and 4 is full professional proficiency. Most Foreign Service jobs that require language require a 3/3 level proficiency, and this level is required in at least one language to achieve tenure, but for first-tour officers, a rating of 2/- in the hard languages (Chinese, Japanese, Russian, etc.) is acceptable. In fact, when I enrolled in the Chinese course, for the first two months we were only taught to speak and understand. When I asked about instruction in reading and writing, I was told that it was too difficult, wasn't required, and therefore was not done for the six-month students. My East Texas stubbornness kicked in, and I raised such a fuss, all the way up to the head of the department, a special exception was made for me, and a couple of the teachers volunteered to teach me to read and write the Chinese ideographic script. Thus, at the end of six months, rather than graduating with a language rating of 2/-, I was awarded a 2/2. In addition, because I'd been exposed to Cantonese in San Francisco during visits to my older brother who lived there, I was able to test in Cantonese Chinese at 1+/2

If, at this point, I'm sounding like something of a troublemaker—I was, and not just when I started language training. I had to make trouble to get my first assignment to the consulate general in Guangzhou, China in the first place. The assignments office had been reluctant to approve my request for the assignment because our two children were eight and nine at the time, and the personnel in that office worried about sending a junior officer (JO) with small children to a post that was considered a hardship (in Guangzhou in 1983, we lived and worked in a hotel, and were under constant surveillance by Chinese authorities). I had to forcefully point out that my children were born abroad when I was in the army, that by the time I retired from the army in 1982, they'd already gone to school in North Carolina, California, and Korea, and were more accustomed to packing and moving, or living under austere conditions than any of my A-100 colleagues. Whether it was because I made a good case, or they just didn't want to argue, Personnel (now HR) caved and the Ray family was off to Guangzhou.

At the end of my 18-month first tour, it was expected that as an Administrative (now Management) cone officer, I would request a second tour in my cone. I was, in fact, offered a couple of jobs in Africa, including one as the principal administrative officer for a small embassy. I'd seen during the brief time I was in Washington that many African-American officers were encouraged to take assignments in Africa, and while there didn't seem to be any overt discrimination, it struck me that it would be a waste of my extensive experience in Asia during my time in the army to send me there, so I didn't include any Africa posts on my onward assignment request.

As luck would have it, an interesting assignment came up about six months before my departure from Guangzhou, and it sounded fascinating; but, it initiated another round of battles with the personnel system.

The officer who'd been deputy consul general in Guangzhou, James Hall, was assigned as the first consul general at a newly opened post in northeast China at Shenyang. Jim and I had had a good relationship in Guangzhou, and our children (he had three girls around the same age as our two) were good friends, and he asked me if I'd be interested in heading the consular section in Shenyang. I, of course, said yes, but the personnel system was apoplectic.

A number of excuses were put forward by the system against the assignment. First, someone said, it was unprecedented to put a second-tour, untenured officer in charge of a section (ignoring the fact that it was done frequently at Africa posts). Another argument was that if I didn't serve in my cone I would find it hard to achieve tenure. Thanks to my own stubbornness, and the firm support from Jim Hall, Ambassador Art Hummel (more about him later), and the DCM, the personnel system once again caved and the assignment went forward. To assuage the concern that I wouldn't be getting experience in my principal cone, in addition to running Shenyang's consular section, I was assigned some administrative duties, becoming in effect, the post's General Services Officer (GSO) and procurement officer. To say that I was busy during my two-plus years in Shenyang would be an understatement, but it was also one of the most interesting and fulfilling of my government jobs.

It was at Shenyang that my interest in the subject of ethics in government was stoked, an interest that led inexorably to this book. It wasn't any single incident that drew me to the subject; rather an accumulation of observations and experiences.

Before I describe the origin of my interest in this subject, allow me to digress and describe, from my perspective, ethics in the Foreign Service, the State Department, and in a sense, the U.S. Government at large.

The Office of Government Ethics (OGE), established by 5 USC, App 4, Sections 401-408, administers the laws and regulations on ethical conduct for all members of the executive branch of government, including employees of the U.S. Department of State (and, this includes the Foreign Service). The statutes and regulations relating to ethical conduct are all compliance related, covering such issues as outside employment, bribery, etc. Some executive branch departments and agencies have supplemental regulations—the Department of State does not.

All State Department personnel are required to undergo ethics training annually, and in addition, certain senior officials or employees in certain positions are required to file annual financial disclosure reports. At the risk of offending those who are responsible for the ethics program, the annual training is little more than a *pro forma* acknowledgment that one has watched a video, or in the early days of my career, read a brochure. The financial disclosure forms are a bit more involved, but as mentioned, they're only completed by a select few individuals. So, in essence, ethics is a once-a-year exercise. As I will make clear later, this is necessary to ensure *compliance* with ethical prohibitions, but hardly sufficient to ensure that an organization's personnel are adequately equipped to navigate the murky waters of those ethical dilemmas when one must choose between two or more 'legal' but perhaps not 'right' courses of action.

What these voluminous laws and regulations do is inform individuals what conduct is prohibited. They rather clearly establish what behavior is illegal. What they do not address are the gray areas where there is no absolute right or wrong. They offer no help to an individual in dealing with the ethical dilemmas.

And, sadly, extensive compliance ethical regulations are often not enough. The case of the energy giant, Enron, is a case in point. In a December 16, 2016 *Harvard Business Review* article, 'Why Ethical People Make Unethical Choices,' by Ron Carucci, it was pointed out that Enron had an ethics and compliance policy that was reviewed and signed annually by all employees. Despite this, employees were caught up in a scandal that ultimately involved even the CEO, and resulted in jail sentences. The annual ethical compliance signature did nothing to prevent the blatant disregard for rules exhibited by Enron's personnel.

One of the reasons given in the article for otherwise good people making bad choices was that 'ethical behavior is not part of routine conversation.' Ethics is seen as something you talk about only when there's been a scandal, or as part of the official compliance program. You get your annual ethics orientation, and like a flu shot, you're good for another year. In the private sector, nearly half of the workforce reports observing ethical misconduct, and a significant percentage report being pressured to compromise ethical standards.

Partially as a result of The Enron and other corporate scandals, resulting in millions of dollars in losses, corporations are beginning to realize that compliance, or rules-based ethics give the illusion of reducing risk without actually doing so.[1]

Ethics has been added as a component to much of the training that government employees receive; at FSI, for example, sessions on ethics are now part of many of the courses, such as the consular and leadership training courses. But, this training still focuses only on compliance ethics.

It would be naïve to assume that the situation in government, or in the Foreign Service, is any different than it is in the private sector, and here we're only talking about the ethical lapses or violations. What of the gray area cases? Is it wise to assume they don't exist? From my own experience and observations, I've concluded that this is precisely what too many people in leadership positions do. They conveniently put their heads in the sand where they can't see, and then assume that if they don't see it, it does not exist. All I can say to people who take that approach is; when your head is in the sand, another part of your anatomy is painfully exposed.

A change to our approach to ethics is long overdue. While we should, understandably, continue to insist that people behave ethically, require periodic orientation, training and certification in compliance with the law and regulations, but we also need to add training on aspirational ethics, or dealing with ethical dilemmas; we need to make ethics a routine part of our workplace conversation.

The focus in ethics needs to be shifted from what we should *not* be doing to what we *should* be doing, from what we *don't* want to be to what we *aspire* to be. The subject of ethics shouldn't be like a trip to the dentist, necessary but unpleasant. We need to stop focusing on the negative aspect of ethics and turn our attention to the positive.

Unfortunately, one of the most significant impediments to changing this mindset exists within the Foreign Service itself. An all-too-common attitude among many in the Foreign Service is that, in the words of AFSA President, Barbara Stephenson, writing in the April 2016 edition of *The Foreign Service Journal,* "The training acquired through assignments is the primary means by which the Foreign Service develops the next generation of leaders." Stephenson went on to point out that more than 70 percent of career development comes from 'a carefully thought out series of assignments, 20 percent from mentoring, and 10 percent from formal training.' Given the lack of sufficient mid-level officers with the requisite experience to be effective mentors, and the fact that in order to get the most out of assignments, inexperienced officers need senior, experienced guidance (mentoring), this is not a reliable way to get any kind of effective training, let alone the required discussions of ethics issues. I would also point out here that the reference was to 'training' and not 'education.' The sad fact is that the Foreign Service and the Department of State do not have a career education system designed to 'build' foreign affairs professionals.

Chapter 1

What are Ethical Dilemmas, and why do they matter?

I've used the terms 'ethical dilemma' and 'ethical lapses or violations' several times up to this point and I've alluded to what I mean by them. In this chapter, I'd like to define them more fully, and explain the importance of the distinctions I make between them.

An ethical lapse, as I use it in this book, is a violation of law or regulation. It's usually easy to see on which side of the ethical line such actions fall. For example, if an ambassador allows his or her spouse to use the ambassador's official vehicle and driver to go to and from a garden club or bridge club meeting, rather than using a personally-owned vehicle (POV), this is, in most cases, a violation of the policy on use of official vehicles. The State Department's Foreign

Affairs Manuals (FAMs) contain various department regulations. 14 FAM 430, Managing Official Vehicles at Posts Abroad, governs the use of official government vehicles, and outlines the exceptions that allow 'other authorized use,' which is a term of art to refer to those occasions when the ambassador or chief of mission has authorized post personnel to use official vehicles for private purposes (usually with reimbursement to the government for such use). These 'other authorized uses,' are ordinarily only when private local transportation has been deemed unsafe or unavailable, or the use is advantageous to the U.S. Government. In this case, unless the ambassador has determined that it would be unsafe to use private or local transportation, and then subsequently reimburses the government for this use, this is a violation of the regulations—and ethical lapse. Furthermore, there are special rules governing the official vehicle assigned for the ambassador's use, which are covered in the Ambassador's Seminar, a two-week orientation course for all first-time chiefs of mission, and I remember from my own time in the class, that this specific example was given as a clear violation of policy.

Ethical dilemmas, on the other hand, are those actions that fall into that gray area where there are no absolute rights or wrongs. These are complex situations arising from conflicts between the moral imperatives or ideology of two people, or the conflict between an individual's moral principles and the demands of the position. Ethical dilemmas are complex situations, involving conflict between moral imperatives, so that to obey one is to violate the other.

Ethical dilemmas arise when values, i.e. personal moral values versus organizational values, conflict, or when there is a conflict between our personal core values and the values expected by our profession.

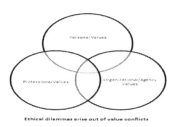

Ethical dilemmas arise out of value conflicts

A 2016 study of corporate executives from India, Colombia, Saudi Arabia, the US, and the UK, showed that they faced numerous ethical dilemmas at work. Of the many dilemmas mentioned in this study, only 16% involved serious issues such as bribery, corruption, or anti-competition. Most, instead, were the result of competing interests, misaligned incentives, and culture clashes.[2]

An example of an ethical dilemma would be ordering an employee not to report on certain activities in a region because this would be received unfavorably in the capital. There's nothing illegal about this, and often it makes a certain amount of sense from the point of view of the person giving the order, since to upset higher headquarters can often have negative consequences. But, failing to report accurately and completely, to enable policy makers to have a full picture of conditions in a country can also have negative consequences; thus, the dilemma.

Choosing between Right and Wrong is often an easy thing to do.

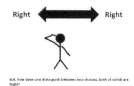
But, how does one distinguish between two choices, both of which are Right?

I don't think it's an exaggeration to say that the vast majority of government employees, including members of the Foreign Service, encounter these gray areas frequently, sometimes unaware of their ethical nature, only that they can often be uncomfortable.

Here are some of the complex situations that create ethical dilemmas:

- Conflict between two professional values – between the moral imperatives of two persons.

Conflict between the moral imperatives of two persons

- Conflict between moral values and the demands of the job.

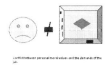
Conflict between personal moral values and the demands of the job.

- Conflict between personal values and professional values.

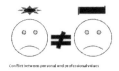

Conflict between personal and professional values

The latter two might seem to be the same thing stated in different ways, but there is actually a difference between them, which I hope the following examples will explain.

The fact is, a number of things impact our ability to act ethically. In the first instance, there is our own sense of morality, or personal values. Then there are some universally-accepted moral values, such as compassion, fairness, respect, and responsibility; the values of our profession and of our organization or department; societal or community values, and, for Americans, Constitutional values. Examples are shown in the following table:

Personal Values	Professional Values	Organizational Values	Constitutional Values	Global Values	Societal or Community Values
Fairness	Technical expertise	Loyalty	Representative government	Compassion	Love of country or community
Honesty	Reputation for excellence	Efficiency	Due process	Fairness	Achievement
Compassion	Objective/truthful reporting	Effectiveness	Separation of powers	Respect	Recognition
Empathy		Collaboration	Equality	Responsibility	
Courage		Goal achievement	Responsiveness		
Loyalty		Stewardship of resources			
Freedom					
Achievement					
Personal responsibility					

A Universe of value systems that can lead to value conflicts, both internal and external.

Each of these sets of values affect individual actions, as shown in this diagram:

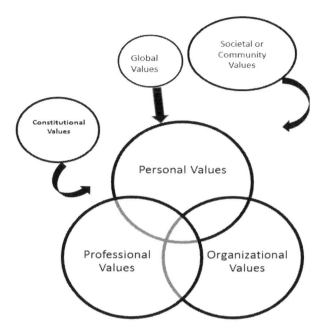

For diplomats there are at least six sets of values that come into play, and conflicts can occur within a set of values as well as between various sets.

I've shown a closer relationship among personal, professional and organizational values for a reason. According to Dr. Jonathan Ingbar, in a monograph prepared for the Institute for Global Ethics, *Organizational Values: Where Values and Cultures Meet*, ethics 'happens in the middle ground between individual moral codes and overarching global values.' It is in this middle ground where the daily interactions and associations occur that a real sense of ethics 'happens.' The real ethical dilemmas occur when personal, professional and organizational values conflict or collide, and sometimes, we have conflicts between values within a set, e.g., a moral belief that it's wrong to kill conflicting with a belief in our responsibility to protect loved ones if they're lives are threatened.

Following is an example of a conflict between and among values; in this case, personal values versus organizational and organizational versus Constitutional.

In 1970, William Watts, then White House Staff Secretary for the National Security Council during the Nixon Administration, resigned his job after an acerbic encounter with Alexander Haig who was Nixon's chief of staff. Watts was strongly opposed to the 1970 invasion of Cambodia, but was basically told by Haig, 'You've had an order from your commander-in-chief, and you can't refuse.' Watts, who felt strongly that his loyalties were to the Constitution and the American people first, disagreed, and walked off his job; a case of personal moral values conflicting with the job at hand, and in this case, personal moral values winning.[3]

The following situation is a fictionalized account based on actual events. In Country X, a local official made a public announcement stating that he would impose new restrictions on foreign non-governmental organization (NGO) operations in his province. Coming at a time when US policy was to support NGO efforts, it was felt that a strong public statement against this action was called for. The American ambassador in Country X, however, disagreed. At the time, an American citizen had been arrested in the governor's province, and the embassy was involved in quiet negotiations to secure his release. The ambassador felt that a public statement condemning the governor's statement (at this point, no further action had been taken) could jeopardize chances of securing the American citizen's freedom and departure from the country, so she declined to make a public statement, which upset those in the bureaucracy in Washington who were pushing for the statement. This was a case of a conflict between personal values and professional values as well as a conflict between two ideologies. The bureaucrats who wanted the statement in support of NGOs were not wrong; rather they were narrowly focused on their area of interest, while the ambassador's focus was on giving priority to the safety of an individual.

In the aforementioned situations, there was no clear line between right or wrong, not even in the first case. While the decision to invade Cambodia in 1970 was questionable on moral grounds, like Truman's decision to use atomic weapons on Japan near the end of World War 2, there was no violation of existing rules of warfare involved. Those involved in the prosecution of the war in Vietnam during this period (and, I count myself among that number) acted and decided based upon the information they possessed at the time. In Truman's case in World War 2, it was the belief that a land invasion of the Japanese home islands would have resulted in far greater casualties, American and Japanese, than were caused by both bombs. The desire in Vietnam in 1970 was to dissuade the North Vietnamese from attacking the south by destroying their safe havens in eastern Cambodia and disrupting the southern terminus of the Ho Chi Minh Trail. Those individuals who felt that we shouldn't have been in Vietnam in the first place, tended to view every military action as 'wrong,' and while there *were* violations of the law of war (the My Lai massacre, for one), objections to the war were more on moral and political grounds than legal.

That fact notwithstanding, there was no end of ethical dilemmas for those involved in the war effort, and many of those conflicts remain unresolved.

The diplomatic service is no different. On a regular basis during my 30-year career I was faced with choices that pitted my personal beliefs and morals against what the organization, or a superior within the organization required or demanded. I had something of an advantage over many of my colleagues who had come to the Foreign Service directly from school or from academia (not, mind you, that ethical dilemmas don't exist in those places as well), in that I had the benefit of 20 years in the military, during which time I'd had the military's ethos of personal integrity drummed into my mind. That, added to the strict upbringing by my grandmother, prepared me to face ethical dilemmas with a better sense of self, the ability and willingness to question so-called authority. When I was faced with situations that fell into the 'gray' area, rather than unquestioningly obey, or refuse outright, I was able to analyze the situation and look for an ethically acceptable (to me) course of action.

Have I always been right? No, and it's probably unreasonable to expect any human to be 100 percent right on anything. I like to think, though, that I was right more than wrong.

There is, however, another reason I believe it's important to understand how to deal with ethical dilemmas. I noticed during my career that there was a depressing tendency for people to 'look the other way' when they encountered people involved in ethical lapses, or to 'wait it out,' and let the offender be transferred to become 'someone else's problem.' This kind of behavior is, to me, the biggest ethical dilemma of all; the question of personal responsibility for the ethical conduct of others. My military training and background taught me that the commander, or person in charge, is responsible for 'everything his or her organization does or fails to do.' Furthermore, every military officer is expected to take appropriate action whenever he or she becomes aware of violations of law, regulation, or proper conduct.[4]

Most, at this point, will be scratching their heads, wondering what I meant in that last paragraph. After all, aren't we responsible only for our own ethical behavior? The answer to that is, of course, is yes and no.

Members of a profession, especially the senior members, are stewards for that profession, responsible for protecting, perpetuating, and preserving its values. This means being responsible for policing the behavior of those members who get out of line. If the Foreign Service is to merit the title 'professional,' then its members must do what all other professions do, and that means learning to effectively deal with ethical dilemmas and with the (hopefully) occasional ethical lapses of its members.

Diplomats are responsible for carrying out the foreign policies developed by the elected political leadership. Given America's historical and cultural antipathy to the profession of diplomacy, an attitude that grew out of the colonial period when diplomats were associated with the monarchies of Europe, and the newly independent United States wanted little to do with it. In fact, Thomas Jefferson, the first American secretary of state, and author of the Declaration of Independence, wrote that 'an independent America had no need of diplomats beyond a few commercial consuls.' The U.S. didn't even send full ambassadors abroad until 1893, and did not establish a career diplomatic and consular service until 1924. Under such conditions, it has always been difficult for the Foreign Service to carry out its responsibilities. In today's political environment, with its hyperpartisan, winner-take-all approach, it is more difficult than ever before.

There are those within the Foreign Service who recognize the need for reform of the way the State Department and Foreign Service approach ethics for diplomats. Edward Marks, a 40-year veteran of the Foreign Service who served as ambassador to Guinea-Bissau and Cape Verde, and is now director of the Simons Center for the Study of Interagency

Coordination, a distinguished senior fellow at George Mason University, and a member of the board of *Diplomacy* magazine, in an article in the July-August 2013 issue of *The Foreign Service Journal,* 'Ethics for the Professional Diplomat,' wrote, 'The belief that civil servants need ethical guidelines arises naturally from their role as professionals who exercise specialized knowledge and skill. As such, they are capable of making judgments, applying their skills and reaching informed decisions in situations that the general public is not qualified to review. How the use of this knowledge should be governed when providing a service to the public can be considered a moral issue, to be managed or regulated by a set of standards or code of ethics . . . a code of ethics is essential to give practitioners guidance with respect of personal, as well as official, boundaries.'

Before it was disbanded, AFSA's Committee on the Foreign Service Profession and Ethics (PEC) commissioned a study through the Institute of Government Ethics (IGE) on the core values ascribed to by members of the U.S. Foreign Service. The survey, conducted in April – May 2013, surveyed over 1,300 Foreign Service personnel (active and retired, in the U.S. and serving abroad). It found that the majority of respondents were vaguely aware of the Department of State core values, but could not name them, and that 70 percent supported having a Foreign Service code of ethics that would provide a foundation for dealing with ethical conflicts, which they viewed primarily as conflicts between the demands of their superiors versus the established rules, and the demands from Washington versus the reality in the field. The complete report on this study can be found at: https://www.afsa.org/sites/default/files/Portals/0/core_values_and_ethical_environment_in_usfs.pdf.

The American political system has never been strong on dealing with nuance or compromise, but the current cadre of politicians demonstrate an unwillingness to compromise, tend to ridicule and show contempt for any they consider opponents, and impugn the motives of anyone who disagrees with them. In addition, from the highest levels in government today, I sense that messages are being sent, whether consciously or unconsciously I cannot say, that encourage unethical behavior. In such an environment, the FSO sent abroad to represent the US who is not clad in the armor of integrity behind a strong shield of ethics will be hard-pressed to live up to the oath to 'support and defend the Constitution of the United States from all enemies, foreign and domestic.'

CHAPTER 2

DEALING WITH ETHICAL DILEMMAS IN DIPLOMACY

In the previous chapter, we discussed what leads to ethical dilemmas. In this and the following chapters we'll look at some of the ethical dilemmas faced by American diplomats, and some suggestions on dealing with them.

During my career, I noticed an almost unconscious tendency among many of my former Foreign Service colleagues to downplay ethical violations by other members of the service unless their actions were really egregious. They are either unnoticed, or treated as aberrations. This 'motivated blindness' is described by Max H. Bazerman and Ann E. Tenbrunsel in an article in the April 2011 issue of *Harvard Business Review,* 'Ethical Breakdowns.' This is a well-documented psychological phenomenon; people 'see what they want to see, and easily miss contradictory information when it's in their interest to remain ignorant.' When it comes to unethical behavior, the tendency is even more pronounced, such as with hiring managers who fail to see or overlook unethical behavior on the part of an employee they were involved in hiring, especially when that behavior contributes to the employee's performance.

Given this situation regarding unethical behavior, I'm forced to think that when it comes to the gray areas, those times when there is no obvious right or wrong, or when it's a choice between two 'rights,' motivated blindness is even more prevalent.

Before looking at some of the kinds of ethical dilemmas faced by diplomats on a daily basis, we'll discuss ways of dealing with them.

Choosing between Right and Wrong is often an easy thing to do.

But, how does one distinguish between two choices, both of which are Right?

IDENTIFY THE DILEMMA

The first step in effectively dealing with these value conflicts is to identify them. It goes without saying that we should first ensure we're not dealing with an ethical violation, where the course of action is clear. Once we've established that we're dealing with an ethical dilemma, it's important to know the precise nature of that dilemma, since not each dilemma is amenable to the same resolution.

You could, as Terry Newell does in his book, *To Serve with Honor: Doing the Right Thing in Government*, use flowchart analysis in identifying the ethical issue with which you're dealing. The following chart is adapted from Newell's book.

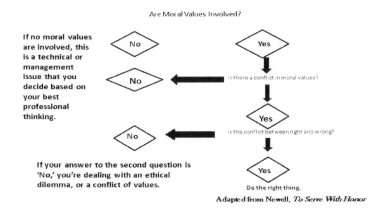

Adapted from Newell, *To Serve With Honor*

Once we've established that we're in a situation of uncertainty, that it's not a matter of legal versus illegal, but rather a conflict between moral imperatives, so that to obey one is to violate the other, we should then determine the nature of that conflict. How we deal with such situations will differ depending upon whether the conflict is internal (conflict between personal and professional values) or external (conflict between personal values and values of another person or the organization). Internal conflicts impact our self-image, while those involving external actors can have financial or career implications.

Dealing with ethical dilemmas

ASSESS OR EVALUATE THE IMPACT OF POTENTIAL DECISIONS

After determining the nature of the dilemma, the next step is to conduct an evaluation of the impact it might have on you, on other people, and on the accomplishment of your mission. The following questions should be asked:

- What are the potential impacts of each course of action?

- Who suffers from each action, and to what degree?

POTENTIAL IMPACTS.

Success in determining the impacts of an action requires the ability to see that issue from viewpoints other than your own.
The questions to be asked are:
- What's at stake for you?
- What's at stake for others involved in the issue?

- What principles are at stake here, and what actions are suggested by those principles?
- What core values are affected by potential actions
    - For you?
    - For others?

Let's take the example of reporting; a political officer has been directed to cease reporting on certain events because senior policy makers are unhappy with the information, and there is a danger that they will reduce funding for the mission if the reporting continues. There are two actions here; 1) stop reporting as directed, or 2) ignore the demand and continue reporting.

1) Notwithstanding the questionable ethics of the senior official who would use the threat of reductions in funding to force a particular action, at the field level, individuals are faced with two choices; acquiesce to the Washington demand, or resist. To acquiesce means that higher-ups are happy and funding is secure, so the mission can continue to work on other equally important goals. It also, unfortunately, creates the possibility that information important to informed policy decisions will not be available at some point in the future. On a personal level, individuals found to be manipulating reporting could be subject to negative performance ratings.
2) Rebuffing the policy maker's 'demand' would ensure the availability of a full range of information to feed into the policy decision making process. It also, though, could mean a reduction in funding that might inhibit the mission's ability to achieve other important goals.

WHO SUFFERS FROM EACH ACTION, AND TO WHAT DEGREE?

It helps to know who benefits from any potential action, but more importantly, when value conflicts are involved, we should endeavor to determine who might suffer, and to what degree.

An exercise often used in ethics courses is as follows:

A Conflict of Values
Do you throw the switch to save the one, or the many?

You're standing near a railroad, next to a shunt switch, and you see a train approaching. Down the track, you see a group of workmen on the main line. They appear to be unaware of the train's approach, and the engineer of the train can't see them as they are around a curve. If the train continues on its current course, it will strike them, probably killing them all. On the siding, on the other hand, one person is standing. He also can't see the train and can't be seen. If the train is switched to the siding, the group will be saved, but the individual will be killed. Do you allow the train to continue on its present course, or do you throw the switch, saving the greater number at the sacrifice of the one?

I'll not give a response, nor do I ask that readers give one. I merely use this example to illustrate the oft-held view that decisions should be made to benefit the many over the few, or to steal a quote from Spock, my favorite *Star Trek* character, "The good of the many outweighs the good of the one." While this view seems to make sense on the surface, it also shows why it's absolutely necessary to carefully analyze the potential impact of your decisions when values are in conflict. What, for instance, would be your decision if the 'one' person on the siding was a famous scientist who was on the verge of making a great discovery that would provide a cure for, oh let's say, cancer? Would it make sense to sacrifice this one person who, in time, could be responsible for saving the lives of millions?

Thankfully, diplomats aren't often put in situations where life or death decisions have to be made—I say, not often, but it *does* happen on occasion—but, the lesson to be taken from this exercise is that all of the elements of a situation must be carefully assessed before making a decision. It's not a matter of one decision being 'right' and the other 'wrong,' but in some circumstances one decision is more 'right.' Some examples of this will be given in the chapter that follows.

In a discussion I had on this subject with a colleague some years ago, it was suggested that the benefits accruing from each course of action should be evaluated, and the action giving the most benefit should be selected. There is, I suppose, some merit to taking this approach, but personally I find an assessment of the harm from actions more in line with my own moral code, and prefer seeking the course of action that does the least harm. This is, of course, a personal preference, and that, in my opinion, is the essence of ethical dilemmas; in the end, each individual must make a choice (decision), and be prepared to live with the consequences of that decision, which leads to the final step in the process:

CHOOSE A COURSE OF ACTION

If you've reached this point in the process, you probably think the rest is easy; simply use your best technical or management knowledge to solve the problem. If only it were that easy.

Before making a final decision, you should be aware that there could very well be subtle biases in your thinking about ethical dilemmas that could be coloring your decision-making process without your awareness. In short, decision making is not an easy thing to do.[6]

After having gone through the identification and assessment process when faced with a conflict of values, it's tempting to think that your decision is rational, and based upon the facts of the situation. This is, however, not always the case. Often, without being aware of it, we make decisions based, not on facts, but on biases, beliefs, or emotions. Let's take the example of the test mentioned earlier in this chapter, where participants had to decide whether or not to throw a switch to allow one person to die in order to save several. In this situation, most participants readily opted to sacrifice the individual by switching the train to the siding, however, when the test conditions were changed, there were different results.

In the variant, instead of two possible routes, there was only one track. The individual was standing on a bridge over the tracks, and the choice to be made was to either allow the train to kill the group of workers, or to push the individual off the bridge into the path of the train. The number of participants who chose to push the individual off the bridge was significantly lower than the number who would switch the train to another track. The logical reasons for sacrificing the one worker to the benefit of the many remained the same, but the thought of deliberately pushing someone to their death was so repellent to participants, the logic was ignored.

There are a number of factors that get in the way of ethical decision making. Some are unique to the individual, but many stem from the organizational culture within which the individual decision maker works. The following is not an all-inclusive list of factors that impede ethical decision making, but it does offer food for thought.

- When core values, of an individual or organization, are forgotten or ignored.
- When an organization creates a 'can-do' attitude that causes individuals to downplay ethics in order to 'get the job done.'
- When ethics violations go unpunished, creating an atmosphere of permissiveness.
- When the hierarchy blocks the flow of information, especially dissenting views.
- When for reasons of hierarchy or specialization, responsibility in the organization is diffused, and ethical problems belong to 'someone else.'
- When there is a pressure to conform, or an attitude of 'go-along, get-along.'
- When an individual in a position of authority pressures an individual to obey orders to perform unethically.
- When individuals at the top of the organizational hierarchy create an atmosphere that encourages unethical behavior.

An example of neglect of core values was the *Challenger* space shuttle disaster, when, on January 28, 1986, the shuttle blew up 73 seconds after launch, killing all seven astronauts on board. The explosion was caused by the failure of an O-ring in the aft field joint of the right solid rocket motor. This wasn't just a freak accident. Problems with the O-rings had been identified before the first shuttle flight in 1981, but the pressure on NASA to keep to its flight schedule was relentless and contributed to a form of bureaucratic blindness to the potential hazard. The possibility of O-ring failure came to be viewed as an 'acceptable flight risk' in order to get the job done. In addition to the tragedy of the loss of seven brave astronauts, including Christa McAuliffe, the first 'teacher in space,' this represented a perversion of NASA's core values:

> Crew Safety
> Mission Effectiveness
> Efficient Use of Resources
> Loyalty to NASA/Chain of Command

In order to meet the aggressive schedule of two launches a month, under a tight budget and increasing pressure from the White House and NASA management, the rank order of NASA's core values seem to have been inverted:

> Loyalty to NASA/Chain of Command
> Efficient Use of Resources
> Mission Effectiveness
> Crew Safety

Relegating crew safety to last place in the organization's value hierarchy doesn't appear to have been a deliberate or conscious decision, but rather, the culmination of bureaucratic pressures. As happens in too many organizations, the core values were known, but no one paid them any attention. (adapted from *To Serve with Honor* by Terry Newell, pp 78-79)

During my 30 years in the Foreign Service, I noticed that many of my colleagues viewed the military, with its mission-oriented focus, as a can-do culture. What they failed, in my opinion, to acknowledge is that the Department of State, suffering from congressional neglect and under-funding for decades, is one of the prime examples of a 'can-do- culture.[7] In a monograph done in association with the Una Chapman Cox Foundation, former Foreign Service Officer (FSO), David T. Jones, described the problems in assigned sufficient numbers of qualified FSOs to staff authorized POLAD positions. Lacking a 'float' of people for long-term education and training like the military has, the Foreign Service is a cadre of people who spend their careers 'rushing as firemen from one blaze to another with never a moment to consider building firewalls, let alone reflecting on better methods of fire prevention. Each time the State Department has achieved funding to hire additional people (ostensibly to build that training float) they have been consumed by the needs of the moment—there's always another fire. This unfortunately leads on occasion to assigning the next available 'warm body' to a position rather than ensuring the individual is a proper match for the assignment. While this is not, *per se*, an ethical lapse, it's easy to see how the press of 'getting the job done' can create conditions making ethical lapses possible. In an article in the March 2013 issue of *The Foreign Service Journal*, 'The Foreign Service Needs a Culture Shift,' I addressed this issue indirectly, in my call for more managed risk taking.[8] While the article didn't address ethics as such, changing the risk-avoidance, go-along, get-along culture of the Foreign Service is a first step in the direction of effectively dealing with ethical dilemmas.

When violations of the rules go unpunished it sends a signal to those within the organization that the rules really don't matter; or worse, if some are punished while others are not, it creates a climate where the prevailing view is that 'who you know' is more important than complying with the rules. During one of my overseas assignments, an individual in the embassy had a relationship with a local which, though it didn't violate any embassy rules or policy, resulted in a public incident. The individual was immediately reassigned, well ahead of the normal end of tour, which was a form of mild punishment. Some months later, another member of the embassy staff became involved in a relationship that did, in fact, violate the ambassador's specific policy. In this case, fearing that the individual would make a legal fuss, the ambassador decided to ignore the violation and allow the individual to complete the normal tour of duty (which, fortunately, only had a few months remaining). While the ambassador's desire to avoid entangling the embassy, and the State Department, in a protracted legal dispute was understandable, these actions sent a signal to others within the embassy community that if one was willing to be an irritant, the rules could be broken with impunity.

In any large organization there are multiple layers of hierarchy through which information must flow. Despite its lack of funding, the Department of State is a multi-layered bureaucracy requiring many in the hierarchy to 'coordinate' or sign off on information flowing both up and down the chain. Added to that, many issues must be coordinated outside State, adding to information-flow impediments. Information can be altered or halted at almost any point in the coordination chain. For example, when I worked in the State Department's Office of Defense Trade Controls in the 1990s, a significant sale by an American company was effectively torpedoed because two offices within the State Department couldn't agree on some relatively minor wording in the memorandum. If important information is blocked going up or down in the bureaucracy, the opportunity for unethical actions is increased.

A joke—sort of—that I remember from the 1960s goes roughly like this; 'when everything is owned by everyone, no one is responsible for anything.' This was a slap at the Communist concept of communal ownership, and an explanation of why things didn't work well in Communist countries. The same thing can be said of bureaucracies where specialization causes a diffusion of responsibility. With the increased specialization in large organizations, and the Foreign Service is no exception to this, the more difficult it is to determine just who is responsible for a given action. The complexity of the tasks facing diplomats today demands a certain degree of specialization, but it also leads to the 'it's someone else's job' excuses that are common when things go wrong. For some within the bureaucracy, specialization puts distance between the individual and the consequences of a given action, which makes it all too easy for unethical behavior to occur. Ethical behavior is more likely when harm is a direct result of actions we take, or we are physically close to those harmed. This was seen in the test involving the train and the workers. When the switch,

> *"Bureaucracy is patriarchy in the extreme, with people being overly cautious, choosing safety over risk, being more interested in self than in service, exercising control for its own sake. No amount of effort to change these qualities around us will be effective until we have confronted these qualities in ourselves. Part of what sustains patriarchy bureaucracy is our own caution, our own wish for safety, our own self-service and desire for control."*
>
> **- from Peter Block, *Stewardship: Choosing Service over Self-Interest.* San Francisco: Berrett-Koehler, 1993, p.40**

which served to distance the test participant somewhat from the consequences of his or her action, was removed, and the prospect of direct action (pushing the individual in front of the train) was introduced, the number of people willing to sacrifice the individual declined dramatically.

Experiments conducted in the 1950s demonstrated that a third of test subjects gave an incorrect answer to a question when other participants (working with the examiner) gave the incorrect answer first, while ninety-nine percent gave the right answer when asked to answer first.[9] When asked later how they could be so off the mark, most answered that they figured the 'majority must be right,' or they didn't want to seem 'inferior to the others even though they believed them to be wrong.' This get-along, go-along attitude exists in all areas of life, but in particular in bureaucracies where advancement can sometimes depend on being considered 'part of the team.'

When hierarchy is added to this mix, things really have the potential to venture into murky ethical areas. As the 1950s experiments demonstrated, the 'pressure to conform' can override independent judgment. When the added pressure of an authority figure is included, the impacts of the aforementioned factors on ethical decision making are multiplied geometrically. Experiments have shown that the average person is predisposed to obey authority figures, even when directed to do something that is thought to be 'wrong.' In at least one known case, the court sided with an organization the punished an employee for failing to do something wrong.[10] The Department of State relieved an employee of his duties and his supervisor gave him a negative performance evaluation for refusing to carry out an assignment that would have violated federal contracting rules. Tim Rainey's supervisor instructed him to require a contractor to rehire a fired subcontractor, which would have violated the Federal

Acquisition Regulation (FAR). When Rainey refused, he was relieved of his contracting duties and given a negative performance rating. Rainey applied to the Merit Systems Protection Board (MSPB) for relief, arguing that the department had inappropriately relieved him of his duties and given him a negative review because he refused to violate federal rules. The MSPB ruled against him, stating that the Whistleblower Protection Act did not apply to him because he had not been ordered to violate a law. The U. S. Court of Appeals for the Federal Circuit upheld the MSPB decision. The court's decision seems to send the signal that an employee can only be protected from retaliation if he or she is asked to specifically violate a federal law. While this court case currently only applies to this specific case, it can't help but have sent chills through the federal workforce. One also has to wonder what message supervisors who might be tempted to order their employees to do something that is ethically questionable got from this decision.

CHAPTER 3

SOME EXAMPLES OF ETHICAL DILEMMAS IN DIPLOMACY

Most of the anecdotes on the following pages, examples of situations that American diplomats face routinely as they perform their duties all over the globe, and are taken from published accounts, and are, thus, public events. Some, though, are from the author's experiences and observations during a 30-year career in the Foreign Service. As these latter are not events known to the general public, and to protect the privacy of the individuals involved, locations and names are not identified. Instead, I've used the technique popular at the State Department's Foreign Service Institute (FSI), and created a fictitious country.

At the end of each anecdote is a list of questions to help the reader analyze the situation. There are no 'right' or 'wrong' answers. Each situation is unique, and each individual brings a different set of values and experiences to the situation.

These are not meant to represent the full range of ethical dilemmas faced by diplomats; that would take a library of books to cover. What they will do, I hope, is cause the reader to think about the situations diplomats face, and how to deal with them.

WHAT IS THE RIGHT THING TO DO?[11]

FSO James W. Spain was in the Foreign Service for 19 years before having to face situations of a choice between god and bad, right and wrong, just and unjust. From 1951 to 1970, as he made his way up the ranks, he assumed such decisions were made by people far above him in the hierarchy. When he was assigned to Istanbul as consul general in 1979, however, a new question entered his day-to-day professional life: What is the right thing to do? He quickly learned that there were no established rules; Washington, usually free with its advice and guidance, was silent on this issue. Here, in his own words, is one of the first ethical dilemmas he faced:

"I had been in Istanbul only a few weeks when I was confronted by the resident U.S. narcotics agent with a proposal to wiretap, without clear cause of court order, the hotel room of a dubious tourist from Los Angeles. Like any Foreign Service Officer, I knew that when it came to local law, the Constitution did not follow an American overseas. But as consul general, I had to conclude that it did travel when it came to relations between Americans. I vetoed the proposal."

DISCUSSION QUESTIONS

1. Was there a conflict of values here? What were they?
2. What would have been the harm if Spain had not vetoed the proposal?
3. Did he make the 'right' decision? Why do you think so?

Inexcusable ignorance[12]

Robert C. Schenck, a native of Ohio, was active in Whig politics and served in the Ohio legislature in 1840, and was elected to the U.S. House of Representatives in 1842, where he served four terms. In 1851, during the administration of Millard Fillmore, Schenck was appointed minister to Brazil. During his two-year stint there, he negotiated trade agreements with Brazil, Uruguay, Paraguay, and the Argentine Confederation. After completing his tour of duty he returned to his legal and political activities in Ohio.

Schenck moved from the Whig Party to the Republican Party, and supported Abraham Lincoln's presidential campaign in 1860. When the Civil War started, Lincoln made him a brigadier general in 1861. While he wasn't particularly adept as a warrior, he was brave, and won promotion to major general for his actions at the Second Battle of Bull Run, where he was severely injured.

In 1863, he returned to the U.S. House of Representatives, serving three terms before losing in 1870. The president at the time was Ulysses S. Grant, who appointed several Civil War military officers (from both sides in the conflict) to ministerial posts. He offered Schenck the post of minister to the Court of St. James, and that's where the Civil War hero and politician went off the rails.

The owners of the Emma Silver Mine in Utah had valued it at $1.5 million, but thought they could sell shares to investors in England for about $5 million. To support their scheme, they ran the mine flat out, selling the silver on the London market (thus, whetting English appetites), but, in the process, exhausting the deposit. They arrived in England shortly after Schenck assumed the post of minister, and invited him to become a member of their newly-formed board of directors, on the assumption that having him on board would demonstrate the 'extraordinary character' of the investment. Along with the position, Schenck was offered an annual payment of $2,500 and a no-interest loan to purchase 10,000 Pound Sterling worth of the mine's stock. Not only would this lend Schenck's prestige to the venture, but it made it appear as if he was a substantial investor as well.

Rather than consult the State Department on the wisdom of accepting this deal, Schenck consulted two colleagues in the embassy who were also former Civil War officers. When neither saw any problems with it, he accepted. After a period of reflection, Schenck had second thoughts, and finally sent a telegram to Secretary of State Hamilton Fish describing the deal and asking for his advice and guidance. Fish immediately cabled back that Schenck should withdraw his name from 'the management of the company,' which he did, but maintained ties to give himself time to sell his shares.

Even though the fraud was eventually exposed, and many people, including Schenck, lost money, he remained in his position as minister for four more years.

After his return to the U.S. in 1876, and partly for political reasons associated with the elections scheduled that year, the House of Representatives launched an investigation of the Emma Silver Mine affair and his role in it. In the report presented to the full House on May 25, 1876, Schenk and Secretary of State Fish were both roundly criticized, but the only punishment recommended by the House was a resolution condemning Schenck for actions that were 'ill-advised, unfortunate and incompatible with the duties of his official position.'

Schenck continued to practice law, but never held a public position again.

DISCUSSION QUESTIONS

While this incident took place during the period of history that saw the political spoils system at its height, it nonetheless offers lessons for the current day.

1. What values were in conflict here? Was this an ethical dilemma; for Schenck? For Secretary of State Fish?
2. Is it reasonable to assume that Schenck, with his legal and political experience, should have known that his actions were unwise, if not illegal?
3. What role did politics play in this incident? Does politics play in ethical dilemmas of the present day?
4. Who was hurt by Schenck's unethical actions?

The good of the many, or the good of the one?

The following is based on an actual incident; names and locations are not shown to protect the privacy of those involved.

Relations between the U.S. and Country X had been strained for nearly a decade when the new American ambassador arrived at post. He was determined to put the bilateral relationship on a more professional footing in order to be able to more effectively protect the interests of American citizens living and working in the country.

About one year into his tour, with only modest improvements in embassy to local government relations, two things happened in one of the country's remote provinces. The provincial governor, an anti-American hardline politician, announced new restrictions on the operations of foreign NGOs operating in his province, restrictions far beyond those imposed by the national government. As this announcement came at a time when totalitarian governments were becoming increasingly restrictive on NGOs, the U.S. position was to react strongly whenever such events occurred. The U.S. reaction, in most cases, was a strong condemnation of anti-NGO actions in a statement issued by the American ambassador. This incident, however, came at the same time that an American tourist in the same province had been arrested on trumped-up, political charges; with provincial authorities threatening to even try the tourist for espionage.

The ambassador faced a dilemma; should he issue a statement condemning the governor's actions against NGOs, which could provoke a negative reaction in the case of the arrested American, or should he forego issuing a statement and focus on getting the American released? The position of the human rights staff in the State Department was that a statement be issued, but in the final analysis, the ambassador has the ultimate authority in such matters.

After serious consideration, the ambassador decided not to issue a statement on the NGO issue, but to respond if queried, and in measured tones at that. He asked the country desk officer to try and block any statement on the specific issue from Washington, at least until the embassy's consular section succeeded in getting the arrested American released and out of the country. In the meantime, he approached senior officials of the provincial governor's political party, outlining both problems and requesting their assistance in resolving them.

A week later, the ambassador's actions bore fruit. Party officials in the capital intervened in the arrest case, and, not only were all charges against the American tourist dropped, but he received an apology and an official escort to the border for his departure. In the case of the NGOs, the governor, under pressure from senior party officials and other governors—assuming his statement wasn't just political posturing in the first place—let the matter drop. In addition, the American NGOs that had been caught up in the issue thanked the ambassador for not intervening, because it could have derailed their own efforts to settle it.

DISCUSSION QUESTIONS

1. *What and whose values were in conflict here?*
2. *What were the ambassador's decision options in this situation?*
3. *Were there any 'right' or 'wrong' decisions in this situation?*

4. Disregarding the fact that, in the end, things worked out satisfactorily for everyone; do you think the ambassador made the 'right' decision?

Taking a calculated risk[13]

My second tour in the Foreign Service was as the sole American consular officer at the newly-opened U.S. Consulate General in Shenyang, China, in the northeast region of China, a consular district larger than Western Europe and Scandinavia combined. I'd been on the job for less than two months when an American businessman was involved in a hotel fire in Harbin, a city in the far north of the consular district, in which several people died, including members of North Korea's government, in Harbin on business.

Under Chinese law, even an accidental fire is treated as a crime if deaths are involved, but the authorities didn't arrest the American right away. They did, however, confiscate his passport and prohibit him from leaving Harbin while the investigation ground slowly on. After nearly a week of basically being confined to his hotel, the man became frantic. He felt isolated and alone, and at the mercy of a bureaucracy whose language and laws he didn't understand. Harbin was a 12-hour one-way train ride from Shenyang, and I had to take care of all the other consular issues (visas, other American citizen service issues) in the district, so I spent weekends in Harbin, and the rest of the week in Shenyang. This was in the days before email and cell phones, and the telephone service in northeast China was so unreliable in 1985, communication between Harbin and Shenyang was problematic, and communicating with the embassy in Beijing or with the State Department in Washington was often out of the question. In other words, it was left to me to deal with this sticky issue on my own.

As this was my second tour in China (the first had been as a junior consular officer in the southern city of Guangzhou), I had a rudimentary understanding of the Chinese justice system, the political system, and, most importantly, the culture. I realized that the officials in northeast China, anxious to attract foreign investment, were reluctant to push the issue of charging and trying an American businessman on such a serious charge, but were also under pressure from authorities in Beijing to uphold Chinese sovereignty and pride. They were, therefore, taking the bureaucratically easy way out; investigating carefully, but restricting the American's movements so that he remained under their control.

While I fully understood what they were doing, and why, I felt that they were violating the individual's right to a fair and speedy hearing, so, with his permission, I decided to take a calculated risk. One day, nearly a month into the situation, during one of my visits to Harbin I informed the local police that when I went to the train station that evening for my trip back to Shenyang, if they hadn't formally charged the American, he would be leaving with me. I knew they wouldn't let him leave, and banked on them not wanting to cause a diplomatic incident by interfering with us in a crowded train station—there was also some international media in the town by this time—and, it turned out to be an accurate assessment. Within 10 minutes of my announcement, the American was formally arrested and charged. The local police were nice about it, though. They placed him under 'house' arrest, allowing him to stay in his hotel under police guard pending trial, and essentially giving him the freedom of the city (of course, with a policeman always nearby).

After that, things moved swiftly. The trial was held four months after the incident, and as expected, he was found guilty, and sentenced to prison. His prison term began in July 1985 after a trial that was widely covered by the international media, and I still traveled to Harbin on a weekly basis to visit him in prison.

While this might sound depressing up to this point, it had a positive outcome. Because his smoking in bed had, in fact, caused the deadly fire, the American pled guilty and asked the court for mercy, something that carries a lot of weight in the Chinese justice system. In prison, he was a model prisoner, and developed a close friendship with the warden, who would occasionally take him to town to see Chinese opera, and whose wife would bake sweets for him frequently. On Thanksgiving Day of that year, just four months after being convicted, I made one final trip to Harbin in connection with this case; to attend the parole hearing for the prisoner. He was paroled for good behavior, immediately released, and welcomed to continue to do business with China.

DISCUSSION QUESTIONS

1. *Are there any value conflicts here? What are they?*
2. *Was I 'right' to take the risk I did?*
3. *What would you have done?*

Dilemmas that diplomats deal with daily

A complete, or even near-complete, list of the behaviors that create dilemmas for diplomats would likely run to thousands of pages. The following list is not to be all-inclusive, but instead, to give a sense of how diplomats have to operate in gray areas, settle value conflicts, and maintain their sanity as they serve the nation's interests. These are some of the more irritating behaviors I observed during my own career, often on a daily basis. While none of them violate any laws—although some come close—they conflict with the values I was taught by my grandmother and those I acquired during a 20-year military career. These are some of the issues that fall in that 'gray area' that is not covered by regulation, nor dealt with in the State Department's training system.[14]

A complete, or even near-complete, list of the behaviors that create dilemmas for diplomats would likely run to thousands of pages. The following list is not to be all-inclusive, but instead, to give a sense of how diplomats have to operate in gray areas, settle value conflicts, and maintain their sanity as they serve the nation's interests. These are some of the more irritating behaviors I observed during my own career, often on a daily basis. While none of them violate any laws—although some come close—they conflict with the values I was taught by my grandmother and those I acquired during a 20-year military career. These are some of the issues that fall in that 'gray area' that is not covered by regulation, nor dealt with in the State Department's training system.[14]

Again, I remind the reader that these issues are not listed in any particular order, not in importance or the degree of irritation they provoke. Different people have different tolerances, and different ideas of the importance of certain behaviors. They are merely intended to give the reader something to think about. I'm reasonably sure that each person viewing this list will have his or her own pet peeves to add, and I encourage that. By recognizing the behaviors we consider to be in the gray area of ethical conduct, we take the first step in ensuring that our own conduct is scrupulous and ethical, and not only avoiding wrongdoing, but all appearance of wrongdoing.

Taking credit for the work of others

FSOs work in a highly competitive environment. Careers hang on the annual Employee Evaluation Report (EER), which is the main document used by promotion boards to decide on advancement in rank. The competitive environment in which FSOs work creates the need to show significant accomplishments on each annual EER, such as unique or notable reporting, creation of a new program, etc. What this often leads to, unfortunately, is a situation where individuals claim credit for work performed by others. Sometimes this might involve reviving an old program at the embassy or consulate and repackaging it as the brainchild of someone currently assigned, or, even worse, having multiple individuals who are currently assigned to an organization claiming credit for the same program or activity.

Sometimes, the sharp eyes of members of promotion panels catch these stratagems, resulting in the individuals involved failing to be promoted. During my 30 years in the Foreign Service, during which time I served several times on promotion panels, I know of no more serious consequences, and I'm sure that in many, if not most, cases, this practice goes undetected or unremarked.

A more insidious form of the practice of taking credit is the supervisor who directs a subordinate to do a job, and then presents the completed job to *his* superiors as his work. It's a fact of bureaucratic and organizational life that the boss always gets the credit for what his or her subordinates do, but it's not meant for those subordinates to be written entirely out of the equation, nor is it meant that the boss claims not only the credit, but that the work is his or hers.

SHIFTING BLAME

If you're the parent of a small child, I'm sure you've experienced this; your child does something bad, like say, breaking your favorite vase. When confronted, the child blames the dog, his sister, or, in extreme cases, an imaginary playmate. Even at an early age, we humans learn the art of passing the buck. Some people grow into adulthood, still incapable of accepting responsibility for their shortcomings. I once dealt with an individual who had blatantly violated several directives from Washington. When he was finally relieved from his job, instead of accepting responsibility for his actions, he blamed his 'incompetent' staff for things going wrong. Years later, when I encountered him, he still did not understand why his tour of duty had been curtailed. This is, admittedly, an extreme example, but anyone who has ever worked in a bureaucracy has, I am certain, encountered similar behavior.

BULLYING, OR ABUSING POSITIONS OF AUTHORITY

For too many people, positions of authority are considered free passes to have their way. Their emphasis, when they're the boss, is being 'bossy.'

Bullying in the workplace takes many forms, from demeaning an employee because of race, gender, handicap, or other trait to undermining an employee's work or placing unreasonable demands. There are no federal laws that apply specifically to bullying, unless the bullying behavior overlaps with discriminatory harassment based on race, national origin, gender, color, age, disability, or religion.

The Department of State has specific policies banning sexual harassment, a pernicious form of gender-based bullying[15] as well as harassment based upon other federally recognized conditions.[16] When the bullying or harassment doesn't fall under one of the protected categories, however, there is no legal or rule-based remedy for the victim. For example, supervisors who yell at or otherwise verbally abuse subordinates across the board, or who otherwise abuse their position of authority, unless *their* supervisor takes action, are not subject to any sanctions. I once worked, for example, for a supervisor who would routinely call me at night, on weekends, or on holidays to fix some glitch he was having with his office computer. No matter how many times I showed him how to either fix the problem himself, or avoid it altogether, the calls continued for a two-year tour, and there was no one for me to turn to for a remedy to the situation.

ACTIONS FOR APPEARANCES RATHER THAN A CONCRETE GOAL

Bureaucrats and politicians want to be seen as 'getting things done.' When that's not possible, or the actions necessary to get something done are too difficult, too dangerous, or just unknown, they perform what I not so generously call 'empty gestures,' gestures for the sake of appearance only, so they can show an audience (voters or someone higher up in the chain of command) that they are 'doing' something.

Sometimes these gestures are as benign as they are meaningless, such as when a bureaucrat convenes a meeting at which attendees spend time discussing a subject, but come to no conclusion. At others, though, the gesture intended to show that something is being 'done' can have a negative impact. Take the public statement, for example. In the *'Good for the many, or good for the one'* case earlier in this chapter, a strongly worded public statement against the provincial official's stance on NGOs wouldn't have stopped him from taking the threatened action, but there were two negative outcomes that have could have resulted. One, it could have provoked him to save face by taking action against the NGOs to show that he wasn't cowed by the U.S. Government, and secondly, it could have caused him to direct the provincial police to take an even harsher line with the arrested American citizen. As the individual whose actions had the potential for the most direct effect on the NGOs and the American citizen, the ambassador on the ground was in the same position as the test subjects asked to consider pushing the individual off the bridge, whereas the bureaucrats in Washington pushing for the strongly worded statement were more akin to the person asked to throw a switch sending the train down the track where it would only kill one person rather than many.

I was once directed to meet with a group of arrested Americans so that the bureau in Washington could brief the Secretary of State that I'd 'met with the arrested Americans and assured them that their situation had high level attention.' The fact that my consular officials were in constant contact with them, and I was being briefed on their case on a daily basis, or whenever anything changed—and, that they were fully aware of this—was of no consequence. The bureaucrats wanted to be able to tell the Secretary, so the Secretary could in turn tell the arrested Americans' hometown politicians, that we were 'doing something.'

Also ignored was the danger that my public intervention in the case could cause the local authorities to dig in their heels—relations between the U.S. and the host country at that time were tense, and the locals were sensitive to what they viewed as American 'bullying.' I managed to finesse the issue, since thankfully the Americans were out on bail, by having the consular officer bring them to a large reception I was holding at my residence for local youth. I greeted each of them as they came through the receiving line, and ensured them that I was keeping a close eye on their case. I was then able to honestly report to Washington that I'd met with them. The case was ultimately settled amicably, without the flurry of media coverage that would inevitably followed my overt involvement in it.

Chapter 4

PUTTING ETHICS INTO ACTION

You've identified the value conflict (ethical dilemma), assessed the impact of various courses of action, and come to a decision. How do you implement your decision?

Every member of the Foreign Service makes a commitment to carry out assigned duties and support government policies, even when they personally disagree with those policies. What happens, though, when there is an irreparable rift between your personal values and the organization's values? Basically, you have three choices: you can remain silent and comply, choosing loyalty to the organization and superiors; you can leave the organization, either quietly, or with a public declaration; or you can voice your disagreement within the organization, and seek a way to resolve the conflict.

Remain silent

The problem with 'going along' is that it changes nothing, and can allow unethical actions to occur. In addition, sacrificing your individual values or integrity can have a corrosive effect on your emotional and even physical health. As an old sergeant major once told me when I was a young army lieutenant, 'the person whose respect I value most is the one staring at me from the mirror when I shave.' Blind loyalty is a slippery slope that, once on, can cause you to slide quickly into the mire of unethical conduct. It can erode your self-respect, and if you fail to respect yourself, you can't expect others to respect you.

Quit

There are two ways to leave an organization when you have an irreconcilable values conflict: 1) leave quietly, or 2) resign or retire with a public statement of the reasons, including media and congressional contacts. There are, though, problems with this choice. One; it's a one-off. You can basically only leave an organization for this reason once, and it's over. Secondly, it also leaves the way open for unethical actions and no change in organizational behavior. Finally, there's always the possibility that your position is wrong, and the organization is right.

Work for change on the inside

Giving voice to your ethical concerns and trying to work for change from within the organization would seem to be the preferable way to deal with situations like this, but as with everything, the devil is in the details.

If you disagree with the decision of your organization or supervisor, you can expect that there will be resistance. Before taking such a step, you should be aware of the tolerance or lack of tolerance for dissent within your organization. The Department of State has the Dissent Channel, which provides an authorized and protected means for employees to express disagreement with policies or procedures, but as with anything, how a specific dissent is received will depend upon the personality of the individuals involved. Before taking the path of internal resistance, do your homework. Is the issue important enough to risk the impact dissenting might have on your career? Are the moral stakes high enough to take such risks? Approach dissent in an objective manner; no finger pointing or personalizing of issues, and don't put your supervisors on the spot by making your dissent public. Don't expect rapid or radical change, if any at all. In fact, it's a good idea to be prepared to fail. If possible, express your dissenting view before a final decision is made. If your dissent fails, accept defeat graciously, and remember, there always the possibility that you're wrong or biased.

If your dissent fails, but you're unable to reconcile the issue with your personal values, you can ask to be reassigned or transferred to avoid having to implement a decision which you morally oppose. If all this fails, you always have the option of leaving the organization (through retirement or resignation, as mentioned above).

Chapter 5

Summary and Recommendations

Effective ethics education is not a 'once-a-year' inoculation like a flu shot. Circumstances change, and sometimes the pressure to 'get the job done' causes people to forget. Laws and regulations are modified, making what was once ethical to be taboo, or vice versa.

For these reasons, exposure to ethics education, and discussion of ethics, must be a regular occurrence in the workplace. Ethical conduct must be modeled by the leadership, and should be a frequent subject of discussion, especially during performance reviews.

While compliance, or rules-based, ethics orientation is important and necessary, it is not sufficient. Ethics education and discussion must also focus on the gray areas of conflicting values; situations when there is no clear-cut right or wrong answer to a problem.

I've used the term ethics 'education' rather than 'training' deliberately. In order to reach the peak of professionalism, diplomats need a system of career education, focused on the core values and concepts of the career, such as that recommended in the American Academy of Diplomacy's report, *American Diplomacy at Risk (ADAR)*, published in April 2015, but I would add to the recommendation contained in that report the need to include education in ethical conduct and dealing with ethical dilemmas as a central component. In addition, *all* training for American diplomats should include ethics as a key element.

As America's representatives to the world; the front line of American security and prosperity; sworn to 'uphold and defend the Constitution,' and to represent what is best about our great country to the world, our diplomats must live and operate by a clear and unambiguous set of standards that are maintained and enforced. In order to do that, they must be provided with all the support and tools they need to succeed.

The following recommendations are based upon my experience, research, observations, and study during a 50-year career in government service. While some of them have resource implications, and will take time and political will to implement, others simply require that we modify the way we currently do business.

RECOMMENDATIONS

1. The Foreign Service Institute (FSI) should develop a certificate program, 'Diplomatic Studies and Practice,' which each new Foreign

Service employee should start in order to achieve tenure. Completion of the program should be required for promotion to FS-01. (ADAR Recommendation 11). In addition, one of the components of this certificate program should be ethics, including dealing with ethical dilemmas.

2. FSI should develop a 'Supervisory Mentoring Course' for mid-level Foreign Service and Civil Service personnel that includes ethical decision making.

3. FSI should develop a course in 'Ethical Decision Making' which should be required for all first-time supervisors, Foreign Service and Civil Service.

4. AFSA and the Department of State should make the following modifications to the Promotion Precepts:

   a. Leadership – Ethical conduct should be specifically mentioned.
   b. Interpersonal – Specify the requirement to conduct oneself in an ethical manner.

5. The annual performance evaluations should address instances of ethical conduct—as positive reinforcement—especially for personnel in leadership positions.

6. The Department should periodically issue guidance on use of the Dissent Channel, ensuring that everyone, from the top down, understands the regulatory basis of this method of expressing disagreement with policy, and reaffirming that no form of reprisal against individuals who make use of the Dissent Channel will be tolerated.

END NOTES

INTRODUCTION

1. 'Corporate Ethics Can't be Reduced to Compliance' by Peter Rea, et al., *Harvard Business Review*, April 29, 2016.

CHAPTER 1

2. 'What You Can Do to Improve Ethics at Your Company' by Christopher McLaverty and Annie

McKee, *Harvard Business Review,* December 29, 2016.

3. 'Take this job and shove it, Mr. Kissinger.' Foreign Affairs Oral History Collection, Association for Diplomatic Studies and Training (ADST), Arlington, VA, http://adst.org/2014/11/take-this-job-and-shove-it-mr-kissinger/.

4. Army Handbook: Life as an Army Officer – the responsibilities, duties, and benefits. July 23, 2014. http://armyhandbook.org/37/life-as-an-army-officer-the-responsibilities-duties-and/.

Chapter 2

5. *To Serve with Honor: Doing the Right Thing in Government* by Terry Newel, pp 27-28.

6. *ibid,* chapter 4, 'Why is Decision Making so Tough?'

7. *The Politico-Military Function and the Department of State* by David T. Jones in association with Una Chapman Cox Foundation, pp 34-35. A monograph assessing the POLAD function in the State Department.

8. 'The Foreign Service Needs a Cultural Shift' by Charles Ray, *The Foreign Service Journal,* March 2013.

9. *To Serve with Honor: Doing the Right Thing in Government* by Terry Newell, pp 84-86.

10. 'Agencies Can Punish Employees Who Refuse to Break Rules,' *FedManager*, June 14, 2016. http://www.fedmanager.com/featured/9-general-news/2499-agencies-can-punish-employees-who-refuse-to-break-rules

CHAPTER 3

11. 'The Right Thing,' by James W. Spain, *The Foreign Service Journal,* October 1982.

12. 'Robert C. Schenck: Political Ambassador and Scoundrel' by Stephen H. Muller, *The Foreign Service Journal,* November 2014.

13. 'Tyranny of Numbers' by Charles Ray, *The Foreign Service Journal,* November 2013.

14. Mak, Dayton and Charles Stuart Kennedy, *American Ambassadors in a Troubled World*, pp. 39-40.

15. Sexual Harassment Policy, U.S. Department of State. https://www.state.gov/s/ocr/c14800.htm

16. Discriminatory Harassment Policy, U.S. Department of State. https://www.state.gov/s/ocr/c24959.htm

BIBLIOGRAPHY

Books

Bennis, Warren, **Old Dogs, New Tricks**, Provo, UT, Executive Excellence Publishing, 1999.

Freedman, David H., **Corps Business: The 30 Management Principles of the U.S. Marines**, New York, HarperBusiness, 2000.

Gupta, Dipak H., **Analyzing Public Policy: Concepts, Tools, and Techniques**, Washington, CQ Press, 2001. (While this is mainly a volume that addresses analytical tools for evaluating public policy, chapters 1, 14, and 15 address the ethical issues as well.)

Hess, Melissa Bayer et al, editors, **Realities of Foreign Service Life, Vol. 2**, New York, iUniverse, Inc., 2007.

Mak, Dayton and Charles Stuart Kennedy, **American Ambassadors in a Troubled World**, Westport, CT, Greenwood Press, 1998.

Maurer, Rick, **Why Don't You Want What I Want?**, Austin, Bard Press, 2002.

Milne, David, **World Making: The Art and Science of American Diplomacy**, New York, Farrar, Straus and Giroux, 2015.

Newell, Terry, **To Serve with Honor: Doing the Right Thing in Government**, Crozet, VA, Loftlands Press, 2015.

Sullivan, Joseph G., editor, **Embassies Under Siege**, Washington, Brassey's, 1995.

Periodicals

The Foreign Service Journal – official publication of the American Foreign Service Association (AFSA).

    October 1982:

        'Lessons in Diplomacy,' page 14
        'The Right Thing,' page 26
        'The Bombing Officer,' page 32

    April 1998:

        'Sierra Leone's Dream,' page 46

    March 2003:

        'The Foreign Service Needs a Cultural Shift,' page 17

June 2013:

'Capitol Hill and Foggy Bottom,' page 18

September 2013:

'The Case for a Professional Foreign Service,' page 56

November 2013:

'The Tyranny of Numbers,' page 45

April 2014:

'Guidelines for Successful Performance as a Chief of Mission,' page 49

July/August 2014:

'How to get Better Ambassadors,' page 17

November 2014:

'A Life of Significance: an interview with Deputy Secretary of State William J. Burns,' page 15

January/February 2015:

'Defining Diplomacy,' page 18
'Teaching Diplomacy as a Process,' page 21

July/August 2015:

'America Needs a Professional Foreign Service,' page 18

'American Diplomacy at Risk: a report from the American Academy of Diplomacy,' page 22

'George Kennan on Diplomacy as a Profession,' page 40

September 2015:

'Deconstructing Dissent,' page 23

'The Value of Military Training for Diplomats,' page 32

September 2016:

''A Foreign Service Trailblazer: Ambassador Ruth A. Davis,' page 24

'When Prevailing Practice Fails: Constructive Dissent,' Page 36

Harvard Business Review

January 6, 2016: 'If You're Loyal to a Group, Does it Compromise Your Ethics?'

April 29, 2016: 'Corporate Ethics Can't be Reduced to Compliance'

Command and General Staff College Foundation News

No. 14/Spring 2013: 'The Ethics of Vicarious Warfare'

Books by this author:

Al Pennyback mysteries
Color Me Dead
Memorial to the Dead
Deadline
Dead, White, and Blue
A Good Day to Die
The Day the Music Died
Die, Sinner
Deadly Intentions
Death by Design
Till Death Do Us Part
Deadly Dose
Dead Man's Cove
Dead Men Don't Answer
Deadly Paradise
Kiss of Death
Death in White Satin
Death and Taxis
Deadbeat
A Deadly Wind Blows
Death Wish
Deadly Vendetta
A Time to Kill, A Time to Die
Dead Ringer
Death of Innocence
Dead Reckoning
Murder on the Menu
Over My Dead Body

The Buffalo Soldier series:
Buffalo Soldier: Trial by Fire
Buffalo Soldier: Homecoming
Buffalo Soldier: Incident at Cactus Junction

Buffalo Soldier: Peacekeepers
Buffalo Soldier: Renegade
Buffalo Soldier: Escort Duty
Buffalo Soldier: Battle at Dead Man's Gulch
Buffalo Soldier: Yosemite
Buffalo Soldier: Comanchero
Buffalo Soldier: Range War
Buffalo Soldier: Mob Justice
Buffalo Soldier: Chasing Ghosts
Buffalo Soldier: The Piano
Buffalo Soldier: Family Feud

Ed Lazenby mysteries
Butterfly Effect
Coriolis Effect
The Cat in the Hatbox

Other fiction
Angel on His Shoulder
She's No Angel
Child of the Flame
Pip's Revenge
Wallace in Underland
Further Adventures of Wallace in Underland
Dead Letter and Other Tales
The White Dragons
The Dragon's Lair
Dragon Slayer
The Last Gunfighters
The Culling
Frontier Justice: Bass Reeves, Deputy U.S. Marshal
Angel on His Shoulder-Revised Edition
Battle at the Galactic Junkyard
Mountain Man
Devil's Lake
Wagons West: Daniel's Journey (from Outlaws Pub.)

Nonfiction
Things I Learned from My Grandmother About Leadership and Life
Taking Charge: Effective Leadership for the Twenty-first Century
Grab the Brass ring
African Places: A Photographic Journey Through Zimbabwe and southern Africa
A Portrait of Africa
There's Always a Plan B
In the Line of Fire: American Diplomats in the Trenches
Advice for the Insecure Writer
Looking at Life Through My Lens
Ethical Dilemmas and the Practice of Diplomacy

Children's books
The Yak and the Yeti
Samantha and the Bully
Molly Learns to Share
Where is Teddy?
Catie and Mister Hop-Hop
Tommy Learns to Count
Catie Goes to School

ABOUT THE AUTHOR

Charles Ray served 30 years in the Foreign Service (from 1982 to 2012), after completing a 20-year career in the U.S. Army. His first Foreign Service assignment was as a consular officer at the U.S. Consulate General in Guangzhou, China. He then served as the sole consular officer at the newly-opened consulate general in Shenyang, China, where he achieved tenure and was reassigned to the Consulate General in Chiang Mai, Thailand, as the administrative officer and acting deputy principal officer.

After three consecutive overseas tours, he returned to Washington where he served as the Special Assistant to the Director of PM Bureau's Office of Defense Trade Controls. After Washington, he went to Freetown, Sierra Leone as Deputy Chief of Mission.

In 1998, he became the first American consul general in Ho Chi Minh City, Vietnam, with consular responsibility for Vietnam from Hue to Phu Quoc Island. In 2002, he became ambassador to Cambodia, serving for three years. During the 2005-2006 academic year he served as diplomat-in-residence at the University of Houston. After leaving that job, he was appointed deputy assistant secretary of defense for Prisoners of War/Missing Personnel Affairs in the Office of the Secretary of Defense, responsible for the recovery, repatriation and